Lost Treasure of the

INCA

LOST TREASURE OF THE
INCA

PETER LOURIE

BOYDS MILLS PRESS
HONESDALE, PENNSYLVANIA

Many thanks to the following photographers:
Eugene Brunner: page 20, 25.
Marcela García: pages 2, 16, 33.
Laura Gillespie: page 14 (right).
Geographico Militar del Ecuador: page 21.
Krisin Hirsch: page 14 (left).
Ron Jones, courtesy of Banco Central of Guayaquil: pages 3, 15, 18, 24.
Ingo Kohler: pages 25, 38, 44.
Library of Congress: pages: 10, 12, 13, 17

Boyds Mills Press, Inc.
815 Church Street
Honesdale, Pennsylvania 18431
Printed in China

Publisher Cataloging-in-Publication Data
Lourie, Peter
        Lost treasure of the Inca / by Peter Lourie.—1st edition.
[48]p. : col. ill. ;   cm.
Summary: Chronicle of an expedition into the Llanganati Mountains of
Ecuador in search of 750 tons of worked gold, which the Incas hid from
the Spanish conquistadors after Pizarro executed the Sun King, Atahualpa.
ISBN 1-56397-7433-5 (hc) • ISBN 978-1-56397-983-5 (pb)
1. Treasure-trove—Ecuador— Juvenile literature.   2. Incas—Juvenile
literature [1. Treasure-trove—Ecuador. 2. Incas.] I. Title.
986.6/ 220 —dc21   1999   CIP
Library of Congress Catalog Card Number 98-88216

First Boyds Mills Press paperback edition, 2001
The text of this book is set in 12-point Clearface Regular.

10 9 8 7 6 5 4 (hc)

10 9 8 7 6 5 (pb)

For my friends
Segundo, Juan, and Washington—
and for Eugene Brunner, the greatest treasure hunter of them all.

—P. L.

ONE

THE TREASURE MOUNTAINS

Over four hundred years ago, the biggest treasure in the world was buried in South America. Eighty miles southeast of Quito, the capital of Ecuador, in a remote chain of mountains called the Llanganatis, lie as much as 750 tons of worked Inca gold. There is strong evidence that the Inca general Rumiñahui hid the gold in this forsaken region when he learned that Pizarro had murdered the Inca Sun King.

For centuries treasure hunters have searched for the gold in vain. Many of them have gotten lost in the cloud forest of the Llanganati Mountains. Some have gone crazy in that haunted place. Others have died there. In spite of the dangers and the odds against them, the treasure hunters keep searching. As the novelist Joseph Conrad once said, "There is no getting away from a treasure that once fastens upon your mind."

When I heard about the gold, I too had to make an expedition into the mysterious treasure mountains. I was hypnotized by stories of adventure. One old treasure hunter in particular said he had discovered where the gold was buried. He said he was about to dig it out. He set me up with his guides so I could make my own journey. But the night before my trek, he cautioned me: "Pete, do you know where you are going? Do you really know? You are going into the beard of the world! Where the fog is alive, like liquid sunshine!"

COLOMBIA

Equator

★ Quito

ECUADOR

Latacunga

Píllaro

Ambato

Triunfo

Llanganati Mountains

Andes Mountains

AMAZON BASIN

PERU

Ecuador is a land of many volcanos. Its mountains are among the highest in South America. My trip would take me to Triunfo, a town deep in the Andes. From there I would head into the Llanganati Mountains in search of a volcano called Cerro Hermoso, where the lost gold is believed to be buried.

The Inca Empire was one of the greatest in history. The map on the facing page shows the empire at its height in 1525 A. D. It ran 2,000 miles down the western coast of South America. The empire encompassed 350,000 square miles, and included present-day Peru, Ecuador, Bolivia, and parts of Colombia, Chile, and Argentina.

The treasure could not be hidden in a better location to foil treasure hunters. The craggy Llanganati Mountains are rugged beyond belief. Cloaked in bewitching fog, they are nearly impassable. To this day the Llanganatis are called "the mountains of electricity and earthquakes" because of the numerous electrical storms and constant earth tremors there. Parts have never been mapped. Aerial photographs often reveal nothing but a vast blanket of cloud.

Most treasure hunters believe the gold was hidden on a fifteen-thousand-foot volcano in the Llanganatis called Cerro Hermoso, or "Beautiful Mountain." To reach the volcano I would have to hike for three days. They said I would encounter snow, rain, sleet, fog, and even earthquakes. The trek would take me through a cloud forest of gnarled jungle so thick it might take days to move only a few miles. Around fourteen thousand feet, I would begin to slog through the high Andean plateau country called *páramo*. The *páramo* of the Llanganatis is littered with quaking bogs—huge clumps of soggy earth floating in muck, a quicksand of marsh and mud.

The treasure hunters also told me about the curse of the Inca—a gold fever that can drive people mad. By feeding the fever, some believe, the Inca people are getting their revenge on the Europeans who murdered their king and conquered their empire.

I caught the fever, all right. I was desperate to see the lost golden birds, the sun disks, and the golden ears of corn. Before my journey, however, I had to learn the history behind the great Inca treasure. I had to know if it was real. I wondered how the gold had gotten into those terrible mountains, and why it had not been discovered earlier.

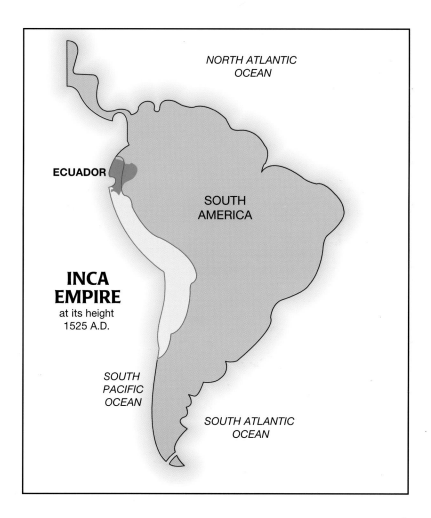

ECUADOR

INCA EMPIRE
at its height
1525 A.D.

NORTH ATLANTIC OCEAN

SOUTH AMERICA

SOUTH PACIFIC OCEAN

SOUTH ATLANTIC OCEAN

The capture of Atahualpa.

TWO

THE RANSOM OF ATAHUALPA

In the early sixteenth century, the Inca empire ran in an unbroken line for two thousand miles along the spine of the Andes, from present-day Colombia in the north to Chile in the south.

By the time of the Conquest led by the Spanish conquistador Francisco Pizarro in 1532, the Incas ruled 12 million people. The Incas called themselves "Children of the Sun." They believed their ruler was divine, for the Lord Inca was descended from the sun, the creator-god. The land, the people, all the gold and silver—everything belonged to the Sun King.

Unlike the Europeans, the Incas valued precious metals not as money but as religious symbols. Gold represented the "sweat of the sun." It was fashioned into exquisite golden ornaments, utensils, goblets, tiles, and plates in honor of their sun god. Silver stood for "tears of the moon" and was fashioned into objects that honored the moon god, sister of the sun. Of all the sacred objects, it is said the most beautiful was the Indian corn—a golden ear sheathed in broad leaves of silver. Also beautiful were the sculpted fountains that sent up sparkling jets of gold while silver birds and golden animals played in the water below.

Atahualpa, the Sun King. The Incas believed he was a direct descendant of the sun—and a god.

These are the prizes that treasure hunters seek in the Llanganati Mountains. They are the precious objects that escaped the hands of the conquistadors, who took everything else.

THE CONQUISTADORS

Inca society was communal and highly structured. The Inca people worked for their families and for the empire as a whole. Only the nobles were educated, and at the top of the society was the Inca king.

Suddenly in 1527 the harmony of the empire was shattered by two brothers, each wanting to be king. A civil war erupted. Huascar, the rightful heir to the throne, ruled the empire from its official capital of Cuzco, in present-day Peru, and his half-brother Atahualpa ruled the northern portion of the empire from Quito, the capital of present-day Ecuador.

In 1532, after a bloody five-year war, Atahualpa finally defeated Huascar and was about to take the throne in Cuzco when Francisco Pizarro and a few hundred Spanish conquistadors landed on the coast of Peru. Atahualpa knew of their arrival but felt confident they could not harm him. He allowed the Spaniards to advance from the coast into the mountains.

Inca runners watched the strangers' every move. They did not realize what kind of enemy was approaching.

Pizarro, with his small army of 62 horsemen and 106 footsoldiers, had come to seize the Inca's gold and silver, to claim the land of the Inca for the king of Spain, and to convert the Indians to Christianity.

In the mountains Pizarro passed Atahualpa's army of eighty thousand Inca soldiers encamped on the hills outside the village of Cajamarca. The royal descendant of the Sun allowed the Spaniards to take up a position in the village. It began to hail, and as night fell Pizarro and his men could see campfires stretching for miles into the distance. Badly outnumbered, the Spaniards feared the worst. But nothing stopped the conquistadors.

THE DEATH OF ATAHUALPA

Pizarro invited the Inca king to meet with him in the village square. This was to be a peaceful meeting. But when Atahualpa came into Cajamarca with six thousand unarmed guards, the Spaniards attacked, killing thousands of helpless Indians and seizing the Inca ruler. Not one Spaniard died in the skirmish.

Atahualpa was immediately imprisoned. The Inca king, dressed in common clothes, now ruled his empire from captivity, but he feared Pizarro would kill him. Noticing the Spaniard's lust for gold, Atahualpa asked to be set free if he could fill a room with the precious metal. The room

Francisco Pizarro murdered Atahualpa and plundered the land of the Inca.

The meeting of two cultures in Cajamarca, Peru: a church built on ancient Inca ruins. It was in this town the Sun King was captured.

Cuzco, Peru, once the capital of the Inca empire.

was twenty-two feet long and seventeen feet wide. He also promised to fill another room twice over with silver. All this he would accomplish in two months' time.

Feverish for loot, Pizarro agreed to set Atahualpa free if he did as he promised. So the Inca king sent messengers throughout the empire to bring his ransom, the ceremonial gold and silver from the temples of the sun and moon. For the next few months the treasure poured into Cajamarca, and the Spaniards melted down the beautiful Inca objects into ingots to be transported back to Spain by ship. But even after roomfuls of gold and silver had been delivered, Pizarro chose not to set Atahualpa free as he had promised.

For two reasons the conquistadors decided to murder the Inca king. First, the Spaniards feared that Atahualpa's most trusted general, Rumiñahui, might attack from the north to free the Lord Inca. Second, Pizarro was anxious to leave Cajamarca in order to ransack all the gold-filled temples throughout the empire. So the Spaniards brought Atahualpa into the square for execution. They fastened him to a pole, and there they strangled the Sun King. Immediately, before Atahualpa's troops could organize a counterattack, the conquistadors set out to raid the Inca temples.

The Treasure of Quito

Pizarro and his men did not know that at the very moment of Atahualpa's death, the greatest treasure in the empire—all the gold from every temple and palace in Quito—was just then being transported south in a last-ditch attempt to free the imprisoned Sun King. A caravan of sixty thousand men bearing the king's ransom, protected by twelve thousand armed guards, was on its way to Cajamarca. Leading the caravan was Rumiñahui himself. Treasure hunters figure that if each load consisted of only 25 pounds of gold, the treasure would weigh no less than 750 tons and would be worth 5 billion dollars in today's money.

When Rumiñahui received news of Atahualpa's murder, he quickly transported the treasure to the Llanganati Mountains, where it could be safely hidden. He was familiar with that difficult terrain because he had grown up in the nearby village of Píllaro.

Rumiñahui was later captured, tortured, and murdered by the Spaniards. But the Inca general never revealed the secret of the treasure. Four centuries later, the gold of Atahualpa lies hidden high in the misty Llanganati Mountains.

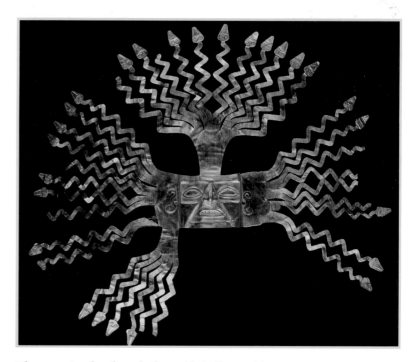

The conquistadors lusted after gold similar to this.

Quito, the capital of Ecuador, where Atahualpa once ruled the northern portion of the Inca Empire.

VALVERDE'S GUIDE

A few years after Pizarro's conquest of the Inca empire, a poor Spanish soldier named Valverde married an Indian woman in Latacunga, a small Andean town near Píllaro, just south of Quito. Her father was a *cacique*, an Indian priest. One day the priest took his new son-in-law into the Llanganatis to find the treasure.

Valverde made many visits into the mountains and became rich. Years later he returned to Spain. On his deathbed he wrote out a three-page guide for the king of Spain—a work known as *El Derrotero de Valverde* or Valverde's Guide—which describes in detail how to reach the treasure in the Llanganati Mountains.

The king of Spain immediately launched an expedition in search of the gold. A Franciscan friar named Father Longo accompanied the expedition into the mountains. For a number of days, the group followed the guide, until one night Father Longo mysteriously disappeared. He wandered off and was never heard from again. After three days searching in the fog for Father Longo, the king's expedition returned to Píllaro without the friar and without the gold.

Even though the expedition had been a failure, one thing had become clear—Valverde's Guide was mostly accurate. Actual landmarks matched the descriptions that Valverde had written out so meticulously for the king. Many years later, however, treasure hunters discovered that the guide grew more confusing toward the end. For four hundred years treasure hunters have been following Valverde's Guide, but sooner or later they get lost in the dense jungle and strange mists of the Llanganatis.

I, too, studied the guide hour after hour before making my own journey. It is a marvelous document. Valverde says that horses must be left behind before hiking on foot to Yanacocha, the black lake, which must be passed on the right. Behind the lake, one must descend a hill to a ravine where there is a waterfall. The next day one will reach another deep, dry ravine, and then come to a mountain of pyrite, or fool's gold, and leave it on the left, passing by in the following fashion ↻.

On the side of a nearby mountain, Valverde says, there will be a pasture in a small plain and a canyon between two hills *"which is the Way of the Inca."* Soon a tunnel will appear *"in the form of a church porch,"* and another waterfall and a quaking bog on the right. There is much gold in the bog, according to the guide. All one has to do is reach in and grab it. Next, ascending the mountain with the bog on the right, one should pass above this second waterfall to find the mouth of a tunnel. The tunnel may be covered by plants, which must be removed in order to enter. There, through that very tunnel, Valverde says, may lie the treasure of the Inca.

The conquistadors plundered the wealth of the Inca. This engraving from 1602 shows Incas, under the command of a Spanish soldier, leading a pack train of llamas carrying silver.

THREE

THE GREATEST TREASURE HUNTER

I first learned about the treasure when I was teaching English in Ecuador. A country the size of Colorado, Ecuador is like a small jewel touching the Pacific Ocean on one side and the Amazon jungle on the other. It sits directly on top of the equator. (Ecuador means equator in Spanish.)

One day in downtown Quito, a crisp mountain town bathed in sunlight, I met an old man named Eugene Brunner. I had heard he was the greatest treasure hunter who ever lived. His reputation, I soon discovered, came not from finding gold, but from searching for it the hardest.

Despite his efforts at treasure hunting, Brunner was a poor man. He had spent all his money on forty-five years of expeditions into the Llanganatis.

I liked Brunner, or Gino, as he asked me to call him, because if he took the treasure out of the mountains, he said he wouldn't keep it for himself. Most of Ecuador's 12 million people are poor, especially those living outside the cities, and Brunner planned to give the treasure to the people of Ecuador.

What really interested Gino about finding the gold was

Eugene Brunner, the greatest treasure hunter of them all.

not the money so much as solving one of the greatest riddles in the world. Gino had come to Ecuador from Switzerland in 1938. Not long after he arrived from Europe, he heard about the Inca gold and decided instantly to make finding the treasure his life's work.

Over the years, he had wandered alone over the *páramo* like a lost soul, with Valverde's Guide in his hand.

By the time I met him, he claimed to have found the actual location of the treasure. He would not tell me exactly where it was, although he did say he'd narrowed it down to a certain area on the volcano, Cerro Hermoso. It was buried under tons of mud, he said, and all that was needed now was the Ecuadorian Army to help him dig the gold out of the mountains.

Over many months in Quito we became good friends. We spent hundreds of hours together at his desk and at cafes. Mostly he told me stories about his expeditions. He also showed me his maps. He had pinpointed the gold somewhere near a small artificial lake. This lake, Brunner said, was made by the Incas when they were mining various metals in the area. He had named the lake Lake Brunner after himself. It was there he had made a camp of thatched huts. It was there he said I could climb with his guides.

I am sure Gino did not think I would find anything. Otherwise he wouldn't have let me go alone. I think he was merely testing me, to see just how good a treasure hunter

Photo of volcano Cerro Hermoso taken from the air. It is a rare occasion when the mountain is free of cloud cover. Lake Brunner, indicated on the photograph, is where it is believed the Incas smelted their gold.

Lake Brunner

The road leading to Triunfo, high in the Andes.

I could become. And he also wanted me to see his camp at 14,500 feet on the edge of the volcano. He was proud of that camp, which had taken him years to build. He said he had supplies up there to last months if the weather got bad.

Triunfo

To reach Lake Brunner near the summit of Cerro Hermoso, I first had to travel by jeep to Triunfo. This small village high in the Andes is the best place to begin a trek into the wild Llanganatis.

Brunner and I drove from Quito for six hours on one-lane dirt roads chiseled into thousand-foot cliffs, up, up, into the mists and moss-drenched trees of the cloud forest, ninety-three hundred feet above sea level.

When we reached Triunfo, barefoot children came out to greet us. Village men in fedoras carried machetes, and women in rubber boots rode donkeys. Mangy dogs lurked in the muddy street. Roosters crowed, and chickens pecked in the cornfields.

Brunner introduced me to the owner of a small store, where I could sleep the night. We drank coffee while the old treasure hunter related a fascinating story.

The valley below Triunfo.

Treasure, such as masks like this, may lie in the Llanganatis.

BARTH BLAKE

Sometime in the last century, one man apparently discovered the treasure. His name was Barth Blake. He and a friend named Chapman followed Valverde's Guide into the Llanganatis. Miraculously, they stumbled upon the gold. But Chapman either died in a fall over a cliff, or, some people believe, was murdered by Blake.

In any event, Blake alone made it out of the mountains. He carried as many pieces of Inca gold as he could fit into his pockets. He went back to England to raise money for an expedition, and was returning over the ocean when someone pushed him overboard to steal his maps.

Before he died, Blake wrote a description of what he had found in the Llanganatis:

"It is impossible for me to describe the wealth that now lies in that cave marked on my map, but I could not remove it alone, nor could thousands of men . . . . There are thousands of gold and silver pieces of Inca and pre-Inca handicraft, the most beautiful goldsmith works you are not able to imagine, life-size human figures made out of beaten gold and silver, birds, animals, cornstalks, gold and silver flowers. Pots full of the most incredible jewelry. Golden vases full of emeralds . . ."

I asked Brunner where those maps were now, but the old treasure hunter just smiled in the dim light of a kerosene lamp. He finished his coffee, and whispered, "Pete, I am sorry, but some things I tell nobody."

Brunner then drove away and left me in Triunfo. After he was gone, I felt so alone. I was frightened about tomorrow's expedition. I slept fitfully until roosters woke me at 4:00 a.m.

Barth Blake left a big clue to the whereabouts of the treasure. In a letter to a friend written in 1887, he said, "Look for the reclining woman and all your troubles are over." Barth Blake saw the "reclining woman" as a landmark. But where was it? Brunner believed he had found the answer. During one of his expeditions, he made a crude sketch of a rock formation. Compare Brunner's drawing with the photo of the mountain. Is this Blake's landmark? Could the "reclining woman" be the volcano Cerro Hermoso? If so, then Brunner was close to the treasure.

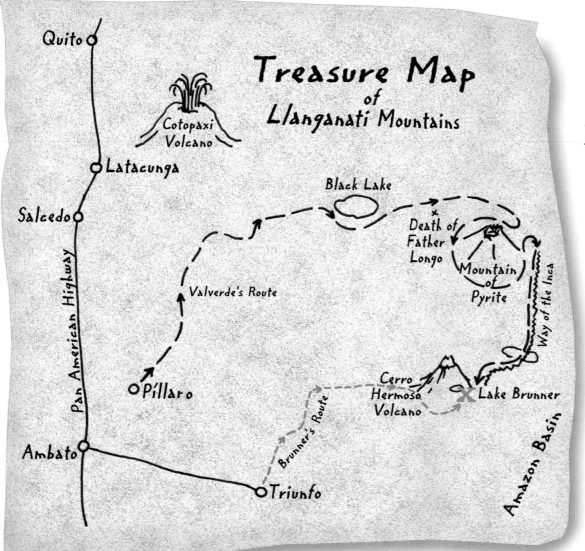

After years of exploration, Brunner found a more direct route than Valverde. This was the route I followed.

FOUR

THE EXPEDITION

Brunner arranged for three of his best guides to accompany me into what he called the "beard of the world." Segundo, Juan, and Washington would carry heavy packs with all our provisions for a week. Brunner had packed rice, Kraft instant dinners, ten cans of tuna fish, *máchica* (a powdered wheat), *piñol* (a raw dark sugar), grease for frying, coffee, tea, and salt. It was so wet in the Llanganatis, everything had to be wrapped in water-tight plastic bags. The supplies would be distributed equally among the men. If for some reason one load fell down a crevasse and was lost, we'd have enough to last us for the hike back to Triunfo.

Segundo would be my head guide. A trim man in his fifties, he had been into the mountains more than 140 times, mostly with Brunner. His calm manner and easy smile put some of my fears to rest. Juan was also a veteran Llanganati guide. He looked like the Incas of old, and he

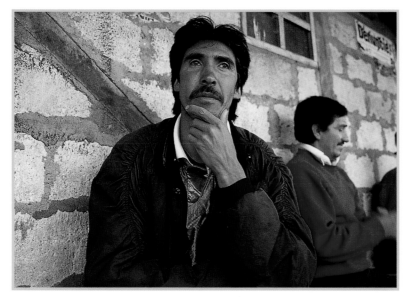

Washington.

Juan and me.

Segundo.

spoke the language of the Incas, which is *Quechua*. He wore a small felt hat, almost too small for his head. Then there was young Washington, moody and brooding Washington. He rarely spoke. All three men could carry heavy loads for hours without drinking water. They never seemed to tire.

With Valverde's Guide in my pocket, we set off in the half-light of the cold dawn. My imagination was filled with stories I'd collected for the past two years. The crowing roosters and barking dogs of town faded into the distance as we followed a lovely green-water stream up a steep slope.

As I walked through the mud trying to keep up with the others, I recalled one story about another expedition leaving for the mountains. The villagers had taunted the treasure hunters. "You will never come back alive," came the voices. The wife of one of the guides cried hysterically as she followed her husband out of town, begging him not to go. Weeks later while deep in the Llanganatis, that very guide became disoriented and fell into a crevasse and died. The following year another expedition of treasure hunters found the guide's body intact, preserved by the mountain cold, lying near a stream.

"Those mountains change people," Brunner told me. He claimed no one had died on any of his own expeditions. But even the greatest of adventurers, he said, can easily become disoriented and irrational in the Llanganatis.

Stories like this raced through my mind as I followed the guides up the mountain, and for the first time I wondered if perhaps Valverde had ever meant to tell anyone where the gold was buried. Perhaps the guide had been written only to foil treasure hunters!

Cowboys from Pillaro rounding up wild horses on the páramo.

THE CLIMB

The morning light was growing stronger, but there was no sun, just the smudge of a gray sky. On such a day only a month before, I had stumbled upon some cowboys near Píllaro. Suddenly in the wilderness I came upon what seemed like a dream—cowboys in the mist rounding up wild horses.

Years later I met cowboys like the ones I saw before my expedition.

Now as I walked with Segundo and the others, I half expected to find these cowboys galloping out of the fog, swinging lassos above their heads. I listened for the pounding hoofs echoing through the lonely Llanganatis. But here, on Brunner's route, there were no people at all. Only mist and jungle and air growing colder and colder as we climbed into the sky.

We climbed from 10,000 feet above sea level to 11,000 feet, and now I was having trouble catching my breath. Washington and Juan moved quickly ahead, but Segundo patiently stayed behind when I had to stop to drink and rest.

After four hours of hard walking, my legs burned with pain. Segundo talked to me the whole time in a soothing voice. I learned he was well respected in Triunfo, and I could see why he was popular. I have never met a kinder man. As I trudged alongside him, he said to me, "Don Pedro, this is a magic mountain we're going to. You might find much more than gold up there."

We followed the stream for hours, but now abruptly we came to a halt. In front of us was a cliff wall, nearly vertical and covered in thick jungle. Segundo lifted his eyebrows and said, "Well, so the work begins. We must climb up there!" And he pointed at the cliff face.

Within minutes he and the others with their heavy packs dove upward into the brush. The hill was so steep I crawled on all fours, through heavy mud. I kept slipping back, then reaching again for vines to drag my limp body upward, inch by inch. Some of the plants were sharp enough to tear my rain gear, but they did not quite reach my skin through two layers of clothing. I struggled every few hundred yards to get enough oxygen. At 13,500 feet above sea level the air was so thin I felt light-headed, as if this were all a dream.

The guides were tireless. Andean peoples are physically well-adapted to mountain terrain. Often while I tried desperately to catch up with them, my guides would simply be waiting for me up ahead.

Because I was having such a hard time, Segundo thoughtfully asked if we should make camp right there on that jungle slope. I said, "Definitely not." And we continued to move slowly forward.

I often heard deep rumbling from the valley below. Segundo said it was earth tremors. Now and then through the vegetation, I could see that we were on a knife's edge of land with the valley falling away on both sides of us.

The climb was physical torture. Then a cloud of mosquitoes attacked me, but not the others. I swatted like a maniac while Segundo laughed. He said the mosquitoes liked to eat treasure hunters; they also liked the color of my beret, which was blue. No sooner had the mosquitoes disappeared than I sat in a nest of biting ants. I had to take off my shirt and pants to slap at more insects.

From my scrapbook: Segundo, Juan, and Washington lead the way.

This wall of vegetation is a good example of the terrain we had to climb.

In the thick jungle, it takes days to move just a few miles.

THE PÁRAMO

After what seemed like endless hours of hard climbing, suddenly we were out of the dense jungle. The sky opened above us like a gray wound, and now we sat on the tabletop of the world. This was the *páramo*.

The *páramo* at 14,000 feet is a boggy, barren, wet, slushy desert. It has its own traps in store for treasure hunters, such as cacti and thorns, but at least now we could see for long distances. We were no longer boxed in by the cloud-covered jungle.

In fact, the sky seemed to swoop down on us. The fog was alive. Unlike fog anywhere in the world, the Llanganati fog moves not in one direction, but in all directions at the same time. For hours it drizzled and sleeted and even hailed a few times as the fog darted madly around the hills and the lakes.

We walked for so many hours I lost count. Finally we came to one of Brunner's thatched camps and I fell onto the straw floor of the hut. Segundo made tea and rice and beans. He brought them to me, but I was queasy with altitude sickness and ate little.

We rose before dawn and set out on the long march through the *páramo*, up brown hills and down brown hills. We saw thousands of little lakes and lagoons and tiny streams. Out of the pearl-gray sky came hailstones the size of nickels. The fog kept rolling like smoke over the desolate land.

The peaks and the distant ridges of the mountains would appear through the mist only suddenly to disappear. Endlessly we slogged through the mud and over the quaking bogs. How, I wondered, did these guides know the way? There seemed to be no path anywhere. They were amazing.

Once or twice the sun came out and turned the streams to silver ribbons and the sky to a shimmering fantasy. It was then I remembered Brunner's description of "liquid sunshine."

Late in the day, Cerro Hermoso stood in front of us, a tower of dark rock, its summit hidden in the brooding clouds. But it was still a long, painful climb to get to Brunner's camp on the volcano's shoulder.

I stopped every few minutes to rub my cramping legs. When I couldn't walk, I crawled up the slope. I kept thinking about all that gold pounded into birds and corn and fountains.

Out of breath, suddenly I spotted four sturdy straw huts around a beautiful, ink-black lake. Here was Lake Brunner!

Moon over the forbidding, but beautiful, páramo.

From my scrapbook: Welcome to "Hotel Brunner."

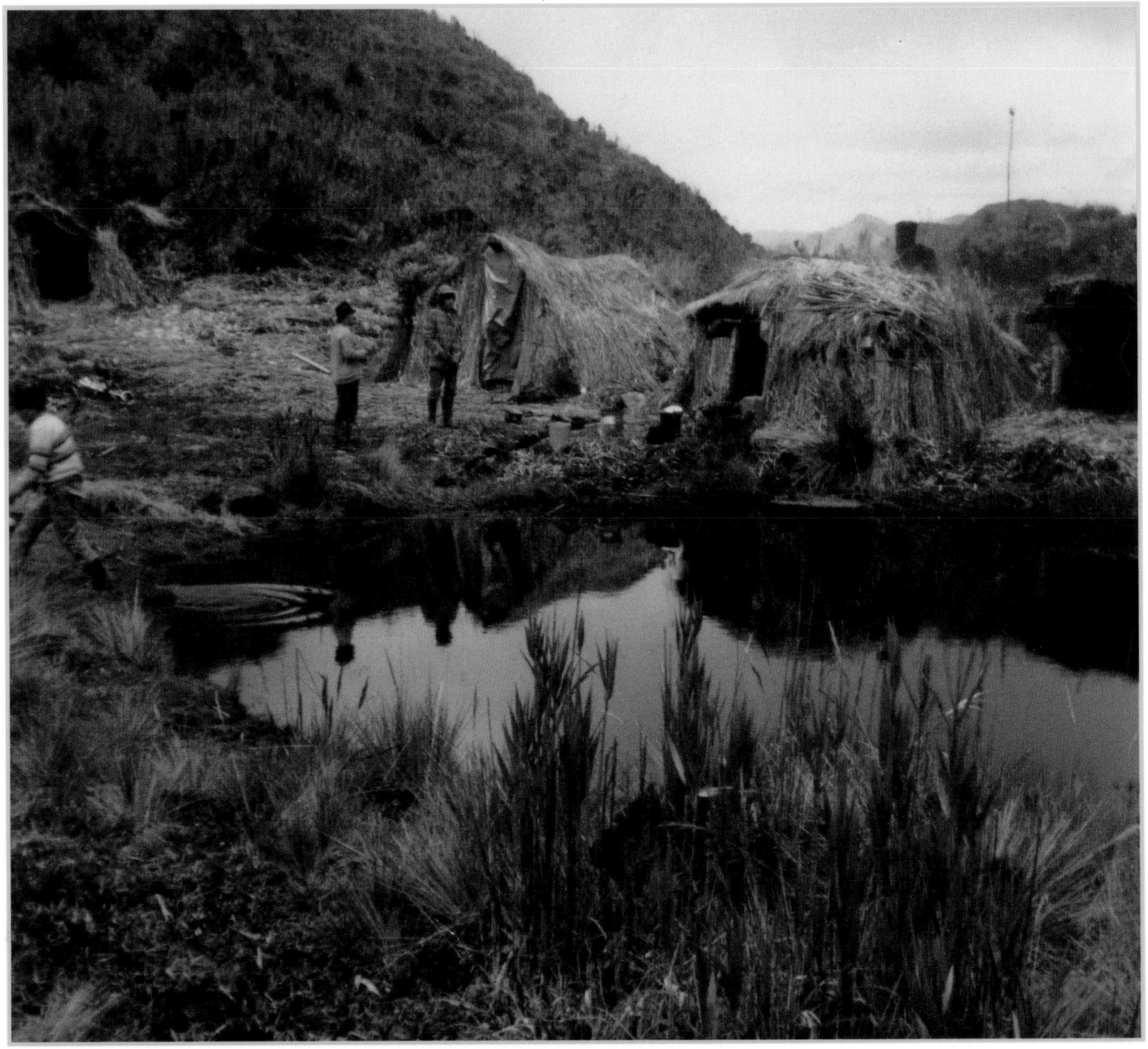

FIVE

LAKE BRUNNER

Segundo, Juan, and Washington were already cooking over a fire. Segundo walked toward me with a cup of hot tea. "Welcome to Hotel Brunner," he said, and he offered me Alka Seltzer to take away the nausea of altitude sickness.

After resting an hour, I walked around camp studying Valverde's Guide. Valverde's voice seemed to echo across the fog as it found its way to me. Everywhere I looked I recognized landmarks that Valverde had described centuries ago for the king of Spain:

"Having come through the canyon and gone a good distance beyond, thou wilt perceive a cascade which descends from an offshoot of the Cerro Llanganati . . . . To ascend the mountain, leave the bog and go along to the right, and pass above the cascade."

That's exactly what we had just done, too. About five hundred feet below camp was a boggy lake with a great waterfall cascading into it from the mountain.

The night came on swiftly. The black wind howled over

Outside one of Brunner's huts.

the *páramo*, and I began to wonder exactly where the treasure might be. Valverde said the gold was hidden in an artificial lake of some sort. So I pulled out the guide.

"Thou shalt perceive the three Cerros Llanganati, in the form of a triangle, on whose declivity there is a lake, made by hand, into which the ancients threw the gold they had prepared for the ransom of the Inca [Atahualpa] when they heard of his death."

Could Lake Brunner itself really be the lake "made by hand"? Was the tunnel nearby and somehow connected to the lake? I now wished Brunner had told me a few more details. He seemed so sure of the treasure's location, but then why hadn't he brought out a few golden birds and ears of corn? Had he ever seen the treasure? No, he couldn't have. Brunner was too poor. Many times I had loaned him money for a meal and the bus home. And besides, he'd said the gold was lying under tons of mud. What did that mean?

Now when I read the guide, I was confused about certain passages: *"And to reach the third mountain, if thou canst not pass in front of the socabón [tunnel], it is the same thing to pass behind it, for the water of the lake falls into it."*

Perhaps Valverde was being intentionally secretive here. After all, he knew well that the Llanganatis are filled with so many nameless mountains and lakes and waterfalls that it is impossible really to distinguish one from another.

I walked around Brunner's camp in the dark but didn't go far for fear of getting lost. I remembered what had happened to Father Longo. I flopped down inside the hut and fell asleep listening to the wind crying and the snow blowing. I dreamed that Valverde was laughing at all the treasure hunters. I tossed in my sleep until dawn.

The morning sun blazed in a deep blue sky, revealing a breathtaking sight—the summit of Cerro Hermoso. But the sight did not last long. Fog rolled in like an ocean wave, so thick it blinded us, and we could not leave our huts. The third day the fog lifted long enough for us to hike up the shoulder of the mountain.

Wherever I walked, I looked for human footprints. Brunner had told me about seeing the barefoot tracks of humans deep in these mountains. He said a lost tribe called the Sabellas lived up here. Legend has it that they were the last survivors of a people who were never conquered by the Spaniards, and have had absolutely no contact with the outside world. The Sabellas were said to be tall and fair-skinned. But no one has ever seen them.

For the next few days I kept an eye out for any sign of the legendary lost tribe, but found nothing—no footprints, no campfire smoke. Often the fog was too thick for exploring. One day I wandered from the hut and began to panic. I realized I was lost in the fog, perhaps only a few yards from safety! Fortunately I stumbled back into camp, and

Segundo making camp.

37

Cerro Hermoso on a rare clear day.

not into the lake. Segundo warned me that I must be more careful.

I had plenty of time to get to know the guides. We played cards and laughed a lot. One night around the fire, Segundo said, "Pedro, there is magic in this place. Do you feel it?"

I did feel the magic. The treasure must be very near. I could almost sense its presence, like a vibration. Maybe we were camped on top of it. Perhaps it was in Brunner's lake, or under a nearby lagoon, or in a tunnel somewhere near the lake. I knew also that if I wanted to find the treasure, it would take decades of exploring the Llanganatis.

During these long, fog-shrouded days in the mountains, I realized my guides themselves were not treasure hunters. They were the direct descendants of the Incas. They had little interest in searching for ceremonial gold. They were content just to be camping here. They loved these mountains, and I could see why.

I began to feel like one of the most fortunate people on the planet. Just to be here among new friends was a gift, a treasure of sorts. After a few days my altitude sickness returned, and much of the time I had little energy. Segundo grew concerned about my health. He said we must leave tomorrow for a lower altitude.

"But I haven't even looked for the gold," I said.

Segundo shook his head with a patient smile. Softly

he said, "Don Pedro, you have made the journey. You have your gold."

Our last night on the mountain, I popped my head out of the hut and found a sky filled with stars. I saw Cerro Hermoso illuminated under the silver glow of moonlight, and I knew I was in the presence of the ancient Incas. Indeed I had been given a gift greater than gold.

The next morning I had a splitting headache. We broke camp under a thick fog. I could hear the roar of the mighty waterfall close by. Segundo watched over me as we came off the mountains, over the bogs and mists of the *páramo*, and down the jungle slope sliding in the dark mud.

As we trudged into Triunfo, I thanked Atahualpa, the Inca Sun King, for letting me witness the mystery of his realm. Later that week in Quito, I thanked Gino, too, and left Ecuador for the United States. It would be many years before I returned to this magic land.

"Don Pedro, you have made the journey. You have your gold."

Triunfo looked much the same as when I last saw it.

SIX

RETURN TO TRIUNFO

When I got to Quito, sadly I discovered my friend Gino Brunner had died. But I drove again to Triunfo. I wanted to see Segundo one more time. The narrow road to the village was the same, with its thousand-foot drops over the edge into nothing but cloud. The high, misty jungle had not been cut, but still dripped with moss and mystery.

As I came into the village, I kept thinking about the old treasure hunter and all his stories. When Brunner died, many of his papers and maps had mysteriously disappeared. And what secrets he knew about the treasure, I figured, had died with him.

Now, years later, here I was, standing beside the same building where I'd slept the night before my journey to Cerro Hermoso. The village had not changed much in sixteen years. Mangy dogs still lurked in the dirt streets. Chickens still pecked in the cornfields. When the sun came

Greeting Segundo after many years.

out, I spotted the nearby snow-capped volcano Tungurahua. It was so clear I felt I could reach out and touch it.

Anxiously I waited for Washington, Juan, and Segundo to gather at the store. I wondered if they had changed.

Washington showed up first. We shook hands, and he introduced me to one of his four children, a ten-year-old girl. When he smiled, he showed a gold tooth.

Next came Juan strolling briskly down the hill from his house above town. He was the same. It was as if I had never left. He wore his little, green hat. Was it the identical hat? He said, "It is like a dream that you have come back, Don Pedro!"

Finally Segundo, who had had to be called down from tending his cows in the hills, was walking toward me. I rushed up to greet him. We shook hands warmly. Except for the graying hair, he looked the same. His face was lively and bright and wise, preserved by the cold mountain air of Ecuador.

Segundo invited me to follow him to his house up the dirt street. We left the others behind. We went inside, and he whispered, "Don Pedro, i found treasure."

On a recent trip into the mountains, Segundo had found a gold object lying in a stream. He now drew a picture of an Inca earring, shaped like a miniature canoe.

"Solid gold!" he said.

"Where is it? Do you still have it?"

"No," he said, "I sold it to some Spaniards."

Segundo paused to study my face. "Alas," he said, "I do not have it."

Before I left Triunfo, I spoke with all three guides. I asked if they would go back with me into the mountains. They nodded yes. They were ready, they said. They would need a week to prepare, that was all.

We shook hands, and I promised to come back soon. But when I drove off, I felt a deep sadness, as if I were leaving my heart behind in that small Andean village. Again I had felt the gold fever—I wanted desperately to make another expedition, perhaps to find some gold in a stream. Yet I

Perhaps one day we will return to the mountains.

realized I had other responsibilities now, a wife and children, a home far away in Vermont.

I'm not sure I'll ever go back again. But even so, I can't stop thinking about Ecuador, the cloud forest, the village, and the *páramo*. Often I dream of taking another journey into the misty Llanganati Mountains. I long to be with those mountain men, camping in the cold rain and the fog like liquid sunshine. Late at night when my children are sleeping and the family dog is running in his sleep, I picture myself traipsing through the beard of the world to the treasure mountains, to that mysterious land of the Inca where the great treasure of the Sun King lies buried still.

VALVERDE'S GUIDE

This verbal treasure map was made by a Spanish soldier who knew where the gold was buried. Since the 16th century, Valverde's Guide has led treasure hunters into the haunting Llanganati Mountains in search of the greatest treasure of all.

Placed in the town of Píllaro, ask for the farm of Moya, and sleep (the first night) a good distance above it; and ask there for the mountain of Guapa, from whose top, if the day be fine, look to the east, so that thy back be towards the town of Ambato, and from thence thou shalt perceive the three Cerros Llanganati, in the form of a triangle, on whose declivity there is a lake, made by hand, into which the ancients threw the gold they had prepared for the ransom of the Inca [Atahualpa] when they heard of his death.

From the same Cerro Guapa thou mayest see also the forest, and in it a clump of *Sangurimas* (trees with white foliage) standing out of the said forest, and another clump which they call *Flechas* (arrow cane), and these clumps are the principal mark for which thou shalt aim, leaving them a little on the left hand.

Go forward from Guapa in the direction and with the signals indicated, and a good way ahead, having passed some cattle-farms, thou shalt come on a wide morass, over which thou must cross, and coming out on the other side, thou shalt see on the left hand a short way off a *jucál* (very tall grass) on a hillside, through which thou must pass. Having got through the *jucál*, thou wilt see two small lakes called "Los Anteojos" (the spectacles), from having between them a point of land like to a nose.

From this place thou mayest again descry the Cerros Llanganati, the same as thou sawest them from the top of Guapa, and I warn thee to leave the said lakes on the left, and that in front of the point or "nose" there is a plain, which is the sleeping-place. There thou must leave thy horses, for they can go no farther.

Following now on foot in the same direction, thou shalt come on a great black lake [Yanacocha], the which leave on thy left hand, and beyond it seek to descend along the hillside in such a way that thou mayest reach a ravine, down which comes a waterfall: and here thou shalt find a bridge of three poles, or if it do not still exist thou shalt put another in the most convenient place and pass over it. And having gone on a little way in the forest, seek out the hut which served to sleep in or the remains of it.

Having passed the night there, go on thy way the following day through the forest in the same direction, till thou reach another deep dry ravine, across which thou must throw a bridge and pass over it slowly and cautiously, for the ravine is very deep; that is, if thou succeed not in finding the pass which exists.

Go forward and look for the signs of another sleeping-place, which, I assure thee, thou canst not fail to see in the fragments of pottery and other marks, because the Indians are continually passing along there. Go on thy way, and thou shalt see a mountain which is all of *margasitas* (pyrite or fool's gold), the which leave on thy left hand, and I warn thee that thou must go round in this fashion ⟲. On this side thou wilt find a *pajonál* (pasture) in a small plain, which having crossed thou wilt come on a canyon between two hills, which is the Way of the Inca.

From thence as thou goest along thou shalt see the entrance of the *socabón* (tunnel), which is in the form of a church porch. Having come through the canyon and gone a good distance beyond, thou wilt perceive a cascade which descends from an offshoot of the Cerro Llanganati and runs into a quaking-bog on the right hand; and without passing the stream in the said bog there is much gold, so that putting in thy hand what thou shalt gather at the bottom is grains of gold.

To ascend the mountain, leave the bog and go along to the right, and pass above the cascade, going round the offshoot of the mountain. And if by chance the mouth of the *socabón* be closed with certain herbs they call "*Salvaje*," remove them, and thou wilt find the entrance. And on the left-hand side of the mountain thou mayest see the "*Guayra*" (for thus the ancients called the furnace where they founded metals), which is nailed with golden nails. And to reach the third mountain, if thou canst not pass in front of the *socabón*, it is the same thing to pass behind it, for the water of the lake falls into it.

If thou lose thyself in the forest, seek the river, follow it on the right bank; lower down take to the beach, and thou wilt reach the canyon in such sort that, although thou seek to pass it, thou wilt not find where; climb, therefore, the mountain on the right hand, and in this manner thou canst by no means miss thy way.

GLOSSARY

Andes: mountain system west South America, extending from Panama to Tierra del Fuego.

Atahualpa: King of the Inca empire at the time of the Conquest. He was held for ransom by the Spanish, but was killed before it was entirely paid.

Barth Blake: British soldier who may have discovered the treasure of Atahualpa.

cacique: local Indian priest.

Cuzco: city in central Peru, formerly the capital of the Inca empire.

Derrotero de Valverde, or Valverde's Guide: a verbal treasure map, written for the king of Spain by Valverde.

Ecuador: a republic in South America situated on the equator above Peru, about the size of the U.S. state of Colorado. Capital is Quito.

Francisco Pizarro: Spanish soldier, conqueror of the Incas. Left Spain an anonymous foot soldier, and came home a fabulously wealthy national hero.

Huascar: Half-brother of Atahualpa and the rightful heir to the Inca throne. Huascar lost the five-year civil war with Atahualpa.

ingot: a mass of metal cast into a convenient shape for storage or transportation to be processed later.

Latacunga: small Ecuadorian town south of Quito.

Llanganati: An Ecuadorian mountain range between the Andes and the Amazon basin.

máchica: powdered wheat staple of the sierra.

páramo: high, wind-swept plateau of the Andes.

Peru: a republic in South America, formerly the center of the Inca empire. Capital is Lima.

Píllaro: small town on the edge of the Llanganati Mountains, birthplace of General Rumiñahu.

piñol: raw dark sugar.

quaking bog: clumps of soggy earth floating in mud and marsh.

Rumiñahui: General in Atahualpa's Inca army. At the news of Atahualpa's death, he fled from the Spaniards, disappearing with the treasure of Quito into the Llanganati Mountains.

Valverde: Spanish soldier who married an Inca woman after the Conquest. Valverde is said to have discovered the gold that Rumiñahui hid in the Llanganati Mountains.

Index

Andes, 8, 11, 22, 47

Atahualpa, 10, 12-16, 36, 39, 45, 47

Blake, Barth, 24-25, 47

Brunner, Eugene (Gino), 19-20, 22, 24-25, 27, 29, 32-33, 36-37, 39, 41

Brunner, Lake, 20-22, 33, 35-36, 38-39

Cajamarca, 13-15

Cuzco, 12, 14, 47

Ecuador, 7-8, 12, 16, 19-20, 39, 41-42, 44, 47

Hermoso, Cerro, 8-9, 20-22, 25, 33, 37-39, 41

Huascar, 12, 47

Inca,
    curse of, 9
    empire, 8, 11-12
    language (*Quechua*) 28

Juan, 27-28, 30, 35, 42

Llangananti Mountains, 7-9, 12, 15-16, 19, 22, 24, 27, 29-30, 36, 38, 44, 47

Longo, Father, 16, 37

parámo, 9, 20, 32-33, 44, 47

Pillaro, 15-16, 29-30, 45, 47

Pizarro, Francisco, 7, 11-16, 47

Quito, 7, 12, 16, 19, 22, 39

Ruminahui, 7, 15, 47

Sabellas, 37,

Segundo, 27, 28, 30-32, 35, 37-38, 41-42

Sun King (Atahualpa), 7, 11, 15, 39, 44

Triunfo, 8, 22-24, 39, 41

Valverde's Guide, 16, 20, 24, 28, 35, 47

Valverde, 16-17, 29, 35-37, 47

Washington, 27-28, 30-31, 35, 42